SANTIAGO

CHILE

TRAVEL GUIDE

2024

An In-Depth Travel Guide to Santiago's Alluring Sights, Exquisite Cuisine, and Unforgettable Adventures in 2024

TABLE OF CONTENTS

SANTIAGO CHILE 2024

INTRODUCTION

Immerse yourself in the captivating city of Santiago, where rich history, vibrant culture, and breathtaking landscapes converge. Join me on a journey through the enchanting capital of Chile, as I share my personal experiences and insider tips to make your visit truly memorable.

From the moment I arrived in Santiago, I was swept away by its dynamic energy and warm hospitality. Stroll through the diverse neighborhoods, each with its own unique charm. Explore Providencia, where trendy boutiques and bustling cafes line the streets. Lose yourself in the bohemian ambiance of Bellavista, where vibrant street art and buzzing nightlife create an electric atmosphere.

Discover the city's rich history as you wander through the historic center, admiring the Plaza de Armas and the magnificent Santiago Metropolitan Cathedral. Immerse yourself in art and culture in Lastarria, where museums, theaters, and charming eateries await. Marvel at the modern skyline of Las Condes, a bustling business district with world-class shopping and dining.

Indulge your taste buds with delectable Chilean cuisine, from traditional dishes bursting with flavors to exquisite seafood delicacies. Explore the local markets, where colorful fruits, vegetables, and artisanal products tempt your senses. And don't forget to savor the renowned Chilean wines with a visit to the nearby vineyards in the Maipo Valley.

For nature lovers and outdoor enthusiasts, Santiago offers a gateway to breathtaking adventures. Embark on exhilarating hikes in the majestic Andes Mountains, relishing panoramic views and pristine landscapes. Or escape to the nearby coastal towns, where golden beaches and refreshing sea breezes beckon.

Throughout this guide, I will provide you with practical advice, insider recommendations, and hidden gems that will help you make the most of your time in Santiago. Whether you're a history buff, an art enthusiast, a food lover, or an adventurer, Santiago has something special to offer.

So pack your bags, and let's embark on an unforgettable journey through the heart and soul of Santiago, Chile's captivating capital. Get ready to immerse yourself in the vibrant culture, indulge in mouthwatering cuisine, and create memories that will last a lifetime. Welcome to Santiago, and get ready to be captivated

CHAPTER ONE
MY TRAVEL EXPERIENCE.

I embarked on a journey to Santiago, Chile, a city that promised a tapestry of captivating experiences and breathtaking moments. The anticipation swelled within me as I boarded the plane, ready to immerse myself in the vibrant culture, rich history, and awe-inspiring landscapes that awaited.

As the plane touched down at Arturo Merino Benitez International Airport, a rush of excitement coursed through me. I stepped out into the warm embrace of Santiago's welcoming atmosphere. The city unfolded before me, a symphony of colors, sounds, and scents that ignited my senses. The adventure had begun.

My first stop was the iconic Plaza de Armas, the heart of Santiago's historic center. Ancient buildings stood tall, exuding the grandeur of bygone eras. The imposing Santiago Metropolitan Cathedral watched over the bustling square, its towers reaching towards the sky. I marveled at the intricate architecture and soaked in the atmosphere, feeling the pulse of the city.

Wandering through the labyrinthine streets, I discovered the diverse neighborhoods that give Santiago its character. Providencia beckoned with its chic boutiques, trendy cafes, and serene parks. Bellavista charmed me with its bohemian vibes, vibrant street art, and hidden corners adorned with local creativity. Lastarria, a haven for artists and intellectuals, captivated me with its museums, theaters, and eclectic dining options.

Interior view ofSantiago Metropolitan Library

One day, I ventured into the surrounding valleys, where vineyards stretched as far as the eye could see. The Maipo Valley, renowned for its wines, offered a glimpse into the art of winemaking. I toured the vineyards, breathing in the fragrant air, and indulged in the velvety flavors of Chilean vintages. Each sip told a story of dedication, passion, and the fertile soil that nurtured the grapes.

Eager to embrace Santiago's natural wonders, I journeyed into the majestic Andes Mountains. Hiking trails carved their way through lush forests, leading me to stunning vistas and pristine lakes. The air grew thinner as I ascended, but the beauty that unfolded was worth every step. I marveled at snow-capped peaks, the jagged edges of the mountains embracing the horizon.

Back in the city, my taste buds danced with delight as I explored the culinary wonders of Santiago. From hearty empanadas filled with savory ingredients to the freshness of ceviche bursting with flavors, every dish tantalized my palate. I delved into local markets, where vibrant produce and aromatic spices created a vibrant tapestry of culinary treasures. Each meal was a celebration of Chilean gastronomy, a fusion of tradition and innovation.

Throughout my journey, the warmth of the Chilean people touched my heart. From the street vendors sharing their stories to the locals who offered a helping hand, the hospitality was genuine and heartfelt. Conversations flowed, laughter echoed through the streets, and connections were forged, bridging the gaps between cultures.

With a heavy heart, I bid farewell to the captivating city of Santiago, but my adventures were far from over. Embarking on a final day trip, I set my sights on Valparaiso, a vibrant port city nestled along Chile's picturesque coast.

As I arrived in Valparaiso, I was immediately enchanted by its bohemian spirit and colorful charm. The hills unfolded before me, adorned with a kaleidoscope of homes painted in vibrant hues. Narrow winding streets led me on a whimsical journey, revealing hidden alleyways and stunning viewpoints at every turn.

Exploring Valparaiso's bustling Cerro Alegre and Cerro Concepcion neighborhoods, I found myself immersed in a world of street art. Vibrant murals adorned the walls, breathing life into the city's rich history and cultural diversity. Each piece of artwork told a story, an expression of the city's soul.

Ascending one of the iconic funiculars, I reached the top of Cerro Artillería. The panoramic view that unfolded before me was simply breathtaking. The vast expanse of the Pacific Ocean stretched endlessly, as if beckoning me to explore its mysteries. Seagulls danced in the air, their calls mingling with the distant sound of waves crashing against the rocky coastline.

Down in the bustling port area, I explored the Mercado Puerto, a vibrant marketplace brimming with local flavors. The enticing aroma of fresh seafood filled the air, drawing me towards a myriad of stalls offering ceviche, grilled fish, and other delectable delicacies. I indulged in a feast of flavors, savoring the unique coastal cuisine that Valparaiso had to offer.

As the day drew to a close, I found solace in the peaceful beauty of the city's Cerro Bellavista. Here, I discovered La Sebastiana, the former home of renowned Chilean poet Pablo Neruda. The house stood as a testament to Neruda's creative spirit, filled with eclectic art, vintage furniture, and sweeping views of the city below. Walking through the rooms, I felt a sense of inspiration and connection to the poet's extraordinary world.

As the sun began to set, casting a golden glow over Valparaiso's hills, I knew it was time to bid farewell to this magical city. The memories I had created in Santiago and Valparaiso would forever hold a special place in my heart. From the vibrant streets of Santiago to the artistic tapestry of Valparaiso, Chile had unveiled its treasures and left an indelible mark on my soul.

As I journeyed back to Santiago one last time, the landscapes unfolded like a mesmerizing painting. The rugged beauty of the Andes Mountains stood tall against the horizon, a majestic backdrop to my cherished memories. I couldn't help but feel grateful for the experiences, the people, and the places that had shaped my journey.

Santiago and Valparaiso had revealed their secrets, inviting me to discover the depths of their charm and allure. As I boarded the plane, I carried with me the spirit of Chile, the vibrant energy of its cities, and the warmth of its people. My adventure had come to an end, but the stories, the laughter, and the memories

I also embarked on a delightful adventure to explore a hidden oasis of colors and fragrances—the Flower Garden of Santiago. Nestled on the outskirts of the city, this enchanting garden promised a captivating display of floral beauty that I simply couldn't resist.

As I entered the garden, I was immediately greeted by a symphony of scents, carried on the gentle breeze. The air was filled with the sweet fragrance of roses, the delicate aroma of lilies, and the invigorating scent of lavender. It was as if nature had crafted a magical perfume just for this garden.

My eyes widened with awe as I beheld the vast array of flowers that sprawled before me. Endless rows of vibrant blooms stretched in every direction, showcasing a kaleidoscope of colors that danced in the sunlight. Shades of red, pink, purple, yellow, and orange painted a picturesque canvas that seemed to come alive with each petal.

Wandering along the garden's winding paths, I marveled at the meticulous arrangements and intricate designs. Immaculate rose bushes stood proudly, their velvety petals capturing the essence of elegance. Delicate orchids, suspended from arches and trellises, added an ethereal touch to the scene. Tall sunflowers reached for the sky, basking in the warm embrace of the Chilean sun.

Every step I took revealed a new floral wonder. Magnificent tulips stood tall in neat clusters, while dainty daisies dotted the landscape with their innocence. Exotic blossoms from around the world mingled harmoniously, creating a harmonious tapestry of diversity and beauty.

As I continued my exploration, I discovered hidden nooks and peaceful corners within the garden. I found a secluded bench beneath a flowering tree, where I could sit and immerse myself in the serenity of the surroundings. The gentle rustling of leaves, the distant chirping of birds, and the distant hum of bees created a soothing symphony that lulled me into a state of tranquility.

Lost in the captivating beauty of the flower garden, I couldn't help but reflect on the power of nature to uplift the spirit and ignite the senses. Each blossom seemed to whisper tales of growth, resilience, and the cycle of life. The garden served as a reminder that amidst the hustle and bustle of city life, nature's wonders were always within reach, offering solace, inspiration, and a profound connection to the world around us.

As the sun began to set, casting a warm golden glow over the garden, I reluctantly bid farewell to this enchanting paradise. The Flower Garden of Santiago had left an indelible mark on my heart, reminding me of the inherent beauty that exists in the simplest things.

Leaving the garden, I carried with me a sense of renewed appreciation for the natural world and a deeper understanding of the harmony that can be found amidst diversity. The memories of that day would forever bloom in my mind, reminding me of the fleeting yet everlasting beauty of flowers and the moments of serenity they gift to those who seek them.

After bidding farewell to the mesmerizing Flower Garden of Santiago, my curiosity led me to embark on another captivating adventure—an excursion to the local zoo. Eager to witness the wonders of the animal kingdom, I set off towards the Santiago Zoo, filled with anticipation and a childlike excitement.

As I entered the gates of the zoo, a world of biodiversity unfolded before my eyes. The air was alive with the sounds of exotic birds, the rhythmic roars of mighty predators, and the gentle chatter of curious onlookers. The vibrant atmosphere was contagious, and I couldn't help but feel a deep connection with the animal inhabitants of this sanctuary.

My first stop was the aviary, a haven for vibrant and elusive bird species. As I strolled through the enclosure, colorful feathers adorned the branches overhead, showcasing nature's artistry. I marveled at the graceful flight of tropical birds, their iridescent plumage shimmering in the sunlight. The melodies of their songs enveloped me, transporting me to distant lands teeming with wildlife.

From there, I made my way to the big cat enclosures. Peering through the glass, I locked eyes with majestic tigers and regal lions, their presence commanding both respect and admiration. Witnessing these magnificent creatures up close, I felt a profound sense of awe and humility. It was a reminder of the delicate balance between humanity and the natural world, urging us to protect and preserve these awe-inspiring species.

Continuing my exploration, I found myself in the company of playful primates. Mischievous monkeys swung from branch to branch, their acrobatic displays leaving me in awe of their agility and intelligence. Observing their intricate social dynamics and expressive gestures, I couldn't help but be reminded of our shared evolutionary roots.

Next, I ventured into the reptile house, where an array of slithering serpents and ancient reptiles awaited. From the mesmerizing patterns of venomous snakes to the prehistoric allure of giant tortoises, I marveled at the diversity and adaptations of these cold-blooded creatures. It was a reminder of the fascinating intricacies of nature and the remarkable resilience of life.

As my zoo expedition drew to a close, I found solace in the tranquil surroundings of the

botanical gardens within the complex. Lush greenery, fragrant blossoms, and tranquil ponds provided a serene escape from the bustling zoo. It was a perfect place to reflect on the profound connection between humans, animals, and the natural world.

Leaving the zoo, I carried with me a renewed appreciation for the wonders of the animal kingdom. The encounters with the diverse creatures had left an indelible mark on my heart, reminding me of the importance of conservation, education, and coexistence. The zoo had served as a gateway to understanding and fostering a deep respect for all living beings that share our planet.

As I walked away, I couldn't help but feel a renewed sense of responsibility to protect these incredible creatures and their habitats. The journey from the Flower Garden to the zoo had been a remarkable tapestry of natural beauty and awe-inspiring encounters—an experience that would forever fuel my passion for wildlife and conservation.

CHAPTER TWO

Essential Travel informations

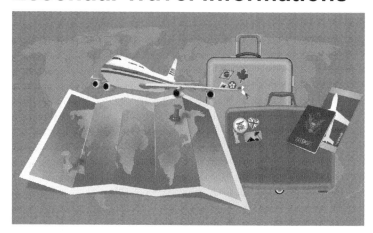

In the months leading up to my much-anticipated journey to Santiago, Chile, I meticulously prepared the essential travel information and documents that would ensure a smooth and unforgettable adventure. With each step, I immersed myself in the excitement of planning and organizing, laying the foundation for a seamless exploration of this captivating destination.

Research became my constant companion as I delved into the intricacies of traveling to

Santiago. I scoured travel websites, read guidebooks, and sought advice from seasoned travelers who had ventured to this vibrant city before. Through their insights and recommendations, I began to shape my itinerary and gather the necessary information to make the most of my time in Santiago.

First and foremost, I ensured that my passport was valid for the duration of my stay and had sufficient blank pages for entry and exit stamps. Knowing that this precious document was the gateway to my adventure, I kept it safely tucked away, ready to be presented at border control upon arrival in Santiago.

Next, I delved into the world of visas and entry requirements. As I discovered that many nationalities, including my own, were eligible for visa-free travel to Chile, a wave of relief washed over me. However, I diligently verified the specific visa regulations for my country of origin, double-checking the length of permitted stay and any additional requirements, such as proof of onward travel or travel insurance.

Equipped with this knowledge, I swiftly moved on to arranging my flights. Comparing different airlines, routes, and fares became a delightful puzzle to solve. After careful consideration, I secured my airline tickets, noting the dates and flight details in my meticulously organized travel folder.

Next on my checklist was travel insurance—a vital safeguard against unexpected mishaps and emergencies. With the assistance of a trusted insurance provider, I selected a comprehensive policy that covered medical expenses, trip cancellation, and lost baggage. I tucked the insurance documents securely in my folder, knowing they would provide peace of mind throughout my journey.

As I delved deeper into the preparations, accommodation choices beckoned. From luxury hotels to cozy guesthouses, Santiago offered an array of options to suit every traveler's taste and budget. After carefully weighing the pros and cons, I selected accommodations that reflected the ambiance and convenience I desired during my stay. Confirming reservations and saving the confirmation details, I completed another crucial aspect of my travel dossier.

To ensure a smooth arrival and departure process, I diligently researched the transportation options available in Santiago. From airport transfers to public transportation within the city, I sought reliable and cost-effective methods to navigate the bustling streets. Armed with maps, schedules, and transportation cards, I felt ready to conquer the city's transportation system with ease.

In the midst of these practical preparations, I also dove into the cultural nuances and local customs of Santiago. I familiarized myself with common phrases in Spanish, the local language, to facilitate communication and show respect to the locals. Additionally, I delved into the rich history, traditions, and etiquette of Chile, eager to immerse myself in the local culture and forge connections with the people I would encounter along the way.

With my essential travel information and documents meticulously organized, I created a travel folder that became my trusted companion. It contained copies of my passport, visa information, flight details, accommodation reservations, travel insurance documents, transportation guides, and notes on local customs and phrases. This folder, neatly tucked away in my travel bag, served as my compass, guiding me through the labyrinth of Santiago and ensuring I was well-prepared for any situation that may arise.

As the day of departure arrived, I felt a mix of excitement and reassurance. The thorough preparations I had undertaken allowed me to embark on my Santiago adventure with confidence, knowing that I had armed myself with the necessary knowledge and documentation to make the most of this extraordinary journey.

With my meticulously prepared travel documents for Santiago, Chile in hand, I embarked on the next step of my journey: organizing and prioritizing the tasks and activities based on the information I had gathered. This allowed me to navigate Santiago with ease and make the most of my time in this captivating city.

First and foremost, I focused on the practicalities of arrival and settling in. Armed with the details of my flight, I ensured that I arrived at the airport with ample time before departure. As I disembarked in Santiago, I followed the immigration procedures, presenting my passport and any necessary visa documentation. The well-organized folder served as a quick reference, allowing me to provide the required information effortlessly.

Once cleared at the immigration checkpoint, I retrieved my luggage and proceeded through customs. Being familiar with the regulations and restrictions beforehand, I smoothly passed through this process, adhering to the guidelines and declarations as needed. With my travel folder in hand, I felt reassured knowing that all necessary documents were readily accessible if required.

As I stepped outside the airport, the next task on my list was transportation to my accommodation. Armed with the knowledge of the transportation options I had researched, I made my way to the designated pick-up points or arranged for a pre-booked transfer service. The details of my transportation arrangements, including addresses, maps, and contact numbers, were readily available in my travel folder, allowing for a seamless transition to my lodging.

Arriving at my accommodation, I presented the reservation confirmation and checked in, settling into my temporary home away from home. With the assistance of the helpful staff, I familiarized myself with the facilities, amenities, and any additional services available. Taking note of the contact information and the establishment's policies, I ensured that I had everything I needed to make my stay comfortable and enjoyable.

With the logistical aspects in order, I turned my attention to exploring Santiago and making the most of my visit. Using the city maps and guides I had gathered during my research, I plotted out the key attractions, landmarks, and cultural sites I wished to experience. The folder, with its wealth of information, served as my compass, guiding me through the city's streets and helping me navigate public transportation routes or arrange for private tours.

Having delved into the local customs and etiquette, I approached each interaction with respect and cultural sensitivity. Armed with some basic Spanish phrases, I embraced the opportunity to engage with the locals, whether seeking directions, ordering at local eateries, or striking up conversations with fellow travelers. The folder contained notes on local customs and phrases, allowing me to navigate social interactions with ease and foster connections along the way.

Throughout my stay, the travel folder served as a valuable resource. I kept it close at hand, ensuring that I had quick access to important documents such as my passport, visa details, and travel insurance information. It also housed any brochures, maps, or vouchers that I collected during my exploration of the city, allowing me to refer to them whenever needed.

As my time in Santiago drew to a close, I reviewed my travel folder, ensuring that all necessary documents and mementos were securely in place. I reflected on the value of thorough preparation and organization, recognizing that my seamless experience in

Santiago was largely due to the careful planning and attention to detail I had invested in the weeks prior.

With a sense of fulfillment and gratitude, I bid farewell to Santiago, knowing that my travel documents and preparations had played a significant role in making my journey a memorable and enriching one. The lessons I learned and the memories I made would forever be cherished, a testament to the power of careful preparation and the wonders that await those who embark on adventures with an organized and informed approach.

Documents needed for travelling

When traveling to Santiago, Chile, there are several documents you may need to ensure a smooth journey. Here is a list of essential documents you should consider:

1. Valid passport: Ensure your passport is valid for at least six months beyond your intended stay in Chile.

2. Visa: Check if your country of citizenship requires a visa to enter Chile. Visit the website of the Chilean embassy or consulate in your home country for visa requirements.

3. Return ticket: Have a copy of your return ticket or proof of onward travel to show your

intention to leave Chile within the allowed period.

4. Entry form: Complete and carry the Tourist Card (Tarjeta de Turismo) form, which you will receive upon arrival in Chile.

5. Proof of accommodation: Carry printed or electronic copies of your hotel reservation or

any other proof of accommodation during your stay in Santiago.

6. Travel insurance: Consider obtaining travel insurance that covers medical expenses, trip cancellation, and personal belongings. Have a copy of the insurance policy readily available.

7. Itinerary: Prepare a detailed itinerary of your trip, including the dates, places you plan to visit, and contact information for accommodations and any tour operators.

8. International driver's license: If you plan to rent a car and drive in Chile, check if you need an international driver's license in addition to your regular driver's license.

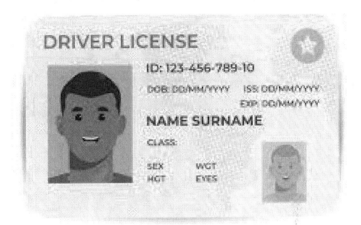

9. Vaccination records: Some countries may require proof of vaccination against certain diseases. Check if any vaccinations are mandatory or recommended for travelers from your country to Chile.

10. Health insurance: While not mandatory, it is advisable to carry proof of health insurance coverage or any specific medical conditions you may have.

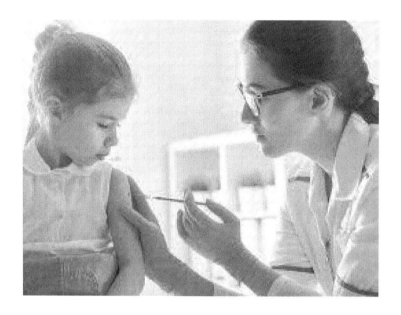

11. Emergency contact information: Carry a list of emergency contact numbers, including your embassy or consulate in Santiago.

12. Currency: Consider carrying some Chilean pesos or have a plan to withdraw money upon arrival. Inform your bank about your travel plans to avoid any issues with your debit or credit cards.

13. Photocopies of important documents: Make copies of your passport, visa, travel insurance, and other essential documents. Keep them separately from the originals as a backup.

14. International mobile phone: Check with your mobile service provider about international roaming options or consider purchasing a local SIM card upon arrival.

15. Prescription medications: If you take prescription medications, carry an adequate supply for your trip and have the prescriptions or doctor's notes with you.

CHAPTER THREE
ACCOMODATIONS

I arrived in Santiago, Chile, with a sense of excitement and anticipation. My accommodation was a charming apartment nestled in the heart of the city, offering a perfect blend of comfort and convenience.

Eager to immerse myself in the vibrant culture, I wasted no time in exploring the city. Armed with a map and a spirit of adventure, I embarked on a journey to discover Santiago's hidden treasures. I started by strolling through the historic streets, marveling at the architectural wonders that lined my path.

Each day brought new experiences and discoveries. I visited the iconic Plaza de Armas, where I watched street performers and admired the grandeur of the Metropolitan Cathedral. The rich history and lively atmosphere left me in awe.

But Santiago had much more to offer than just its city center. I ventured into the bohemian neighborhoods, such as Bellavista and Lastarria, where I immersed myself in the local art scene. I explored charming art galleries, perused trendy boutiques, and enjoyed the cozy cafes that dotted the streets. Every corner seemed to hold a story waiting to be discovered.

Of course, no trip to Santiago would be complete without sampling the delicious cuisine. I indulged in traditional Chilean dishes like mouthwatering empanadas and flavorful ceviche. The local markets, such as Mercado Central, became my go-to spots for fresh seafood and delectable treats. The blend of flavors and aromas was a true delight for my senses.

Santiago's natural beauty also beckoned me. I took a day trip to the stunning Valle Nevado ski resort, nestled amidst the majestic Andes Mountains. The exhilaration of skiing down the powdery slopes, surrounded by breathtaking views, was an experience I would cherish forever. The tranquility of nature provided a perfect escape from the city's hustle and bustle.

Back in the apartment, I found solace and relaxation after long days of exploration. The cozy ambiance welcomed me each evening, offering a space to unwind and reflect on the day's adventures. I enjoyed sipping a cup of local Chilean wine while overlooking the city lights from the balcony, allowing the vibrant energy of Santiago to sink in.

As my time in Santiago drew to a close, I realized that I had truly made the most of my accommodation. It had been the perfect base from which I had embarked on countless adventures, allowing me to delve into the city's rich culture, savor its flavors, and witness its breathtaking landscapes.

Leaving Santiago, I carried with me a heart full of cherished memories and a deep appreciation for the experiences I had enjoyed. The story of how I spent my accommodation well in Santiago, Chile, was etched in my mind, forever reminding me of the beauty and warmth this incredible city had to offer.

Top 100 Best Accomodations in Santiago Chile
1. The Singular Santiago

2. Hotel Santiago

3. The Ritz-Carlton, Santiago

4. W Santiago

5. Hotel Plaza San Francisco

6. Lastarria Boutique Hotel

7. Hotel Altiplanico Bellas Artes

8. Hotel Cumbres Lastarria

9. Luciano K Hotel

10. Hotel Magnolia

11. Hotel Boutique Castillo Rojo

12. Le Rêve Boutique Hotel

13. Hotel Boutique Bidasoa

14. Hotel Ismael 312

15. Hotel Loreto

16. Hotel Bidasoa

17. Hotel Orly

18. Hotel Boutique Tremo

19. Hotel Paris Londres

20. Hotel Isabella Boutique House

21. Hotel Torremayor

22. Hotel Montecarlo Santiago

23. Hotel San Cristobal Tower

24. Hotel Fundador

25. Hotel Boutique Le Reve

26. Hotel Sommelier Boutique

27. Hotel Stanford Santiago

28. Hotel Boutique Reyall

29. Hotel Boutique Tremo Parque Forestal

30. Hotel Montebianco

31. Hotel Bonaparte

32. Hotel Boutique Su Merced

33. Hotel Boutique Le Reve

34. Hotel Galerias

35. Hotel La Casona

36. Hotel Boutique Bellavista

37. Hotel Loreto

38. Hotel Fundador

39. Hotel Casa Lyon

40. Hotel Neruda Express

41. Hotel Menorca Rent a Suite

42. Hotel Diego de Almagro Providencia

43. Hotel Plaza El Bosque Nueva Las Condes

44. Hotel Los Españoles Plus

45. Hotel Manquehue Las Condes

46. Hotel Atton El Bosque

47. Hotel DoubleTree by Hilton Santiago - Vitacura

48. Hotel NH Collection Plaza Santiago

49. Hotel Atton Vitacura

50. Hotel Plaza El Bosque Ebro

51. Hotel Sheraton Santiago

52. Hotel NOI Vitacura

53. Hotel Eurotel Providencia

54. Hotel Kennedy

55. Hotel Eurotel El Bosque

56. Hotel Atton Las Condes

57. Hotel Plaza El Bosque San Sebastian

58. Hotel InterContinental Santiago

59. Hotel Hyatt Place Santiago/Vitacura

60. Hotel Boulevard Suites

61. Hotel Regal Pacific Santiago

62. Hotel NH Collection Plaza Santiago

63. Hotel Plaza El Bosque Nueva Las Condes

64. Hotel Renaissance Santiago

65. Hotel Crown Plaza Santiago

66. Hotel Novotel Santiago Vitacura

67. Hotel La Fayette

68. Hotel Hilton Garden Inn Santiago Airport

69. Hotel Director Vitacura

70. Hotel Four Points by Sheraton Santiago

71. Hotel Radisson Ciudad Empresarial

72. Hotel Best Western Premier Marina Las Condes

73. Hotel Manquehue Aeropuerto

74. Hotel InterContinental Santiago

75. Hotel Atton Vitacura

76. Hotel Cumbres Lastarria

77. Hotel Mercure Santiago Centro

78. Hotel Holiday Inn Santiago - Airport Terminal

79. Hotel Plaza El Bosque Ebro

80. Hotel Sheraton Santiago

81. Hotel NOI Vitacura

82. Hotel Plaza San Francisco

83. Hotel Time Select

84. Hotel BMB Suites

85. Hotel InterContinental Santiago

86. Hotel Galerias

87. Hotel Ismael 312

88. Hotel Novotel Santiago Vitacura

89. Hotel Kennedy

90. Hotel Plaza El Bosque San Sebastian

91. Hotel Eurotel El Bosque

92. Hotel Atton Las Condes

93. Hotel Manquehue Las Condes

94. Hotel Director Vitacura

95. Hotel Eurotel Providencia

96. Hotel Hilton Garden Inn Santiago Airport

97. Hotel Four Points by Sheraton Santiago

98. Hotel NH Collection Plaza Santiago

99. Hotel Regal Pacific Santiago

100. Hotel Crowne Plaza Santiago

Addresses of the Hotels

1. The Singular Santiago - Merced 294, Santiago, Región Metropolitana.

2. Hotel Santiago - Av. Presidente Kennedy 4601, Santiago, Región Metropolitana.

3. The Ritz-Carlton, Santiago - El Alcalde 15, Las Condes, Santiago, Región Metropolitana.

4. W Santiago - Isidora Goyenechea 3000, Las Condes, Santiago, Región Metropolitana.

5. Hotel Plaza San Francisco - Alameda 816, Santiago, Región Metropolitana.

6. Lastarria Boutique Hotel - Coronel Santiago Bueras 188, Santiago, Región Metropolitana.

7. Hotel Altiplanico Bellas Artes - Pío Nono 290, Santiago, Región Metropolitana.

8. Hotel Cumbres Lastarria - José Victorino Lastarria 299, Santiago, Región Metropolitana.

9. Luciano K Hotel - Merced 84, Santiago, Región Metropolitana.

10. Hotel Magnolia - Huérfanos 539, Santiago, Región Metropolitana.

11. Hotel Boutique Castillo Rojo - Constitución 195, Santiago, Región Metropolitana.

12. Le Rêve Boutique Hotel - Orrego Luco 023, Providencia, Santiago, Región Metropolitana.

13. Hotel Boutique Bidasoa - Los Conquistadores 2060, Providencia, Santiago, Región Metropolitana.

14. Hotel Ismael 312 - Ismael Valdés Vergara 312, Providencia, Santiago, Región Metropolitana.

15. Hotel Loreto - Loreto 170, Recoleta, Santiago, Región Metropolitana.

16. Hotel Bidasoa - Avenida Pedro de Valdivia 292, Providencia, Santiago, Región Metropolitana.

17. Hotel Orly - Pedro de Valdivia 027, Providencia, Santiago, Región Metropolitana.

18. Hotel Boutique Tremo - Cienfuegos 51, Barrio Italia, Providencia, Santiago, Región Metropolitana.

19. Hotel Paris Londres - Londres 54, Barrio Paris-Londres, Santiago, Región Metropolitana.

20. Hotel Isabella Boutique House - Las Hortensias 370, Providencia, Santiago, Región Metropolitana.

21. Hotel Torremayor - Ricardo Lyon 25, Providencia, Santiago, Región Metropolitana.

22. Hotel Montecarlo Santiago - Avenida Ricardo Cumming 250, Santiago, Región Metropolitana.

23. Hotel San Cristobal Tower - Josefina Edwards De Ferrari 100, Providencia, Santiago, Región Metropolitana.

24. Hotel Fundador - Paseo Serrano 34, Santiago, Región Metropolitana.

25. Hotel Boutique Le Reve - Orrego Luco 023, Providencia, Santiago, Región Metropolitana.

26. Hotel Sommelier Boutique - Santa Magdalena 91, Providencia, Santiago, Región Metropolitana.

27. Hotel Stanford Santiago - Ricardo Matte Pérez 021, Santiago, Región Metropolitana.

28. Hotel Boutique Reyall - Santa Magdalena 36, Providencia, Santiago, Región Metropolitana.

29. Hotel Boutique Tremo Parque Forestal - Paseo Dimalow 166, Bellavista, Santiago, Región Metropolitana.

30. Hotel Montebianco - Padre Mariano 69, Providencia, Santiago, Región Metropolitana.

31. Hotel Bonaparte - Avenida Cristobal Colon 5620, Las Condes, Santiago, Región Metropolitana.

32. Hotel Boutique Su Merced - Merced 858, Santiago, Región Metropolitana.

33. Hotel Boutique Le Reve - Orrego Luco 023, Providencia, Santiago, Región Metropolitana.

34. Hotel Galerias - San Antonio 65, Santiago, Región Metropolitana.

35. Hotel La Casona - Don Carlos 289, Providencia, Santiago, Región Metropolitana.

36. Hotel Boutique Bellavista - Antonia López de Bello 0125, Recoleta, Santiago, Región Metropolitana.

37. Hotel Loreto - Loreto 170, Recoleta, Santiago, Región Metropolitana.

38. Hotel Fundador - Paseo Serrano 34, Santiago, Región Metropolitana.

39. Hotel Casa Lyon - Av. Ricardo Lyon 217, Providencia, Santiago, Región Metropolitana.

40. Hotel Neruda Express - Av. Pedro de Valdivia 164, Providencia, Santiago, Región Metropolitana.

41. Hotel Menorca Rent a Suite - Menorca 1130, Las Condes, Santiago, Región Metropolitana.

42. Hotel Diego de Almagro Providencia - Avenida Providencia 110, Providencia, Santiago, Región Metropolitana.

43. Hotel Plaza El Bosque Nueva Las Condes - Av. Manquehue Norte 656, Las Condes, Santiago, Región Metropolitana.

44. Hotel Los Españoles Plus - Los Españoles 2539, Providencia, Santiago, Región Metropolitana.

45. Hotel Manquehue Las Condes - Av. Manquehue 656, Las Condes, Santiago, Región Metropolitana.

46. Hotel Atton El Bosque - Roger de Flor 2770, Las Condes, Santiago, Región Metropolitana.

47. Hotel DoubleTree by Hilton Santiago - Vitacura - Avenida Vitacura 2727, Las Condes, Santiago, Región Metropolitana.

48. Hotel NH Collection Plaza Santiago - Av. Vitacura 2610, Las Condes, Santiago, Región Metropolitana.

49. Hotel Atton Vitacura - Alonso de Córdova 5199, Vitacura, Santiago, Región Metropolitana.

50. Hotel Plaza El Bosque Ebro - Av. El Bosque Norte 0124, Las Condes, Santiago, Región Metropolitana.

Santiago, Chile offers a wide range of accommodations to suit various budgets and preferences. The exact number of accommodations available can fluctuate as new properties are built and existing ones undergo changes. However, Santiago is known for its extensive hotel infrastructure, and there are numerous hotels, guesthouses, hostels, and serviced apartments throughout the city. From luxury hotels in upscale neighborhoods to budget-friendly accommodations in central areas, travelers can find options that meet their needs. To get an accurate count of the current accommodations in Santiago, it's recommended to consult reputable travel websites or contact local tourism authorities.

CHAPTER FOUR
Time to visit

As the plane touched down on the runway of Santiago International Airport, I felt a surge of excitement coursing through my veins. The long-awaited adventure to Santiago, Chile had finally begun. Stepping out into the warm embrace of the Chilean sun, I inhaled deeply, taking in the tantalizing scent of unfamiliar spices and the promise of new experiences.

My journey through Santiago unfolded like the pages of a captivating novel, each chapter revealing a different facet of this vibrant city. From the moment I set foot on its bustling streets, I was greeted by the harmonious blend of modernity and history, where towering skyscrapers stood shoulder to shoulder with ornate colonial buildings.

Wandering through the heart of Santiago, I found myself immersed in the bustling energy of the city center. The Plaza de Armas, the beating heart of Santiago, drew me in with its lively atmosphere. Here, I marveled at the grandeur of the Metropolitan Cathedral, its intricate architecture a testament to the city's rich cultural heritage. Nearby, the imposing facade of the Palacio de la Moneda stood as a symbol of Chile's political history, casting a watchful eye over the bustling square.

As the days unfolded, I ventured beyond the city center to discover Santiago's hidden gems. The bohemian neighborhood of Bellavista beckoned me with its vibrant street art, quirky cafes, and eclectic boutiques. I strolled along

Pio Nono Street, soaking in the artistic flair that adorned every corner. The scent of freshly brewed coffee filled the air, enticing me to pause and savor the local flavors while engaging in conversations with the friendly locals.

Escaping the urban buzz, I sought solace in the natural wonders that surround Santiago. A trip to the majestic Andes Mountains was an absolute must. The towering peaks, adorned with blankets of glistening snow, served as a backdrop to my unforgettable adventures. I embarked on a scenic hike, marveling at the breathtaking vistas that unfolded with every step. The crisp mountain air invigorated my senses, reminding me of the awe-inspiring power of nature.

Another day, I ventured to the nearby Casablanca Valley, a wine lover's paradise. Rolling vineyards stretched as far as the eye could see, their emerald green hues dancing in the sunlight. I delved into the world of winemaking, touring vineyards, and tasting the exquisite flavors that have made Chilean wines renowned worldwide. Sipping a glass of Carménère, the signature Chilean varietal, I savored the harmony of flavors that unfolded on my palate, a true testament to the country's viticultural prowess.

Santiago's culinary scene captured my heart and palate, enticing me with a diverse array of flavors and aromas. From traditional empanadas to tantalizing seafood dishes, each bite was a celebration of Chile's culinary heritage. I indulged in fresh ceviche, a symphony of tangy citrus and succulent seafood, and sampled the comforting warmth of a hearty bowl of cazuela, a traditional Chilean stew. Every meal was an opportunity to explore the rich tapestry of Chilean cuisine, leaving me craving for more.

But it wasn't just the sights, sounds, and flavors that made my time in Santiago memorable. It was the warmth and hospitality of the Chilean people that truly touched my heart. From the enthusiastic conversations with locals eager to share their stories to the genuine smiles that greeted me at every turn, I felt a deep sense of connection and belonging.

As the sun began to set on my time in Santiago, I reflected on the countless moments of awe, discovery, and connection that had woven themselves into the fabric of my journey. Santiago had opened its arms and revealed its treasures, inviting me to embrace its vibrant spirit and immerse myself in its rich tapestry of history, culture, and natural wonders.

Leaving Santiago, I carried with me cherished memories, a newfound appreciation for the beauty of Chile, and a promise to return someday. Santiago had become more than a destination—it had become a part of me, forever etched in my heart as a chapter of my life's grand adventure.

Time to visit Santiago

The best time to visit Santiago, Chile largely depends on your preferences and the activities you wish to engage in during your trip. Santiago experiences a Mediterranean climate with distinct seasons, offering different experiences throughout the year. Here are some considerations for each season:

1. Spring (September to November): Spring in Santiago is a delightful time to visit, with mild temperatures, blooming flowers, and vibrant foliage. It's a great time for outdoor activities, exploring the city's parks, and enjoying the pleasant weather.

2. Summer (December to February): Summer in Santiago brings warm to hot temperatures, perfect for exploring the city's outdoor attractions and nearby coastal areas. However,

it is also the peak tourist season, so expect larger crowds and higher prices.

3. Autumn (March to May): Autumn in Santiago is characterized by cooler temperatures and beautiful foliage as the leaves change color. It's a great time for exploring vineyards, enjoying cultural festivals, and experiencing the stunning fall scenery.

4. Winter (June to August): Winter in Santiago brings cooler temperatures, occasional rain, and even snow in the surrounding mountains. It's an ideal time for winter sports enthusiasts who want to hit the slopes, and you can also

take advantage of lower hotel rates during this season.

The months of September to November and March to May offer mild weather, fewer crowds, and opportunities to witness the beauty of spring or autumn in Santiago. However, keep in mind that the city's climate can be unpredictable, and it's always a good idea to check the weather forecast before your trip.

Consider your personal preferences, the activities you wish to engage in, and any specific events or festivals you would like to attend when choosing the best time to visit Santiago, Chile.

CHAPTER FIVE
PLACES TO VISIT

As I embarked on my adventure in Santiago, Chile, I found myself immersed in a world of captivating sights, sounds, and experiences. The city's rich cultural heritage and breathtaking landscapes unfolded before me, offering a tapestry of memorable places to explore and discover.

My journey began in the heart of Santiago's historic center, where the Plaza de Armas beckoned me with its vibrant energy. The iconic Metropolitan Cathedral stood proudly, its intricate facade bearing witness to centuries of history. Inside, I marveled at the grandeur of the cathedral, its lofty arches and ornate altars casting a solemn ambiance that filled me with a sense of reverence.

Leaving the plaza behind, I ventured into the vibrant neighborhood of Bellavista, known for its bohemian charm and artistic spirit. Its colorful streets were adorned with vibrant murals and street art, a testament to Santiago's thriving art scene. Quirky cafes, lively bars, and eclectic boutiques lined the cobblestone lanes, inviting me to indulge in the local flavors and immerse myself in the creative energy that permeated the air.

As I journeyed deeper into the city, I discovered the captivating charm of the Lastarria neighborhood. Its picturesque streets were lined with restored mansions, now housing art galleries, boutique shops, and charming cafes. The scent of freshly brewed coffee filled the air, guiding me to cozy corners where I savored each sip, my taste buds awakened by the rich flavors of Chilean brews.

Beyond the city center, the majestic Andes Mountains loomed, beckoning me to explore their awe-inspiring beauty. I ventured into the Cajón del Maipo, a breathtaking natural wonder just outside the city. The rushing waters of the Maipo River carved through the rugged terrain, while snow-capped peaks towered above. I embarked on a thrilling hike, the crisp mountain air invigorating my senses and the stunning vistas rewarding every step.

No visit to Santiago would be complete without a journey into the nearby wine regions. In the Casablanca Valley, I found myself amidst rolling vineyards, their emerald green vines stretching as far as the eye could see. I indulged in wine tastings, savoring the unique flavors and aromas of Chilean wines, from the elegant whites to the robust reds. Each sip carried the essence of the region's terroir, a testament to the passion and craftsmanship of Chilean winemakers.

For a touch of serenity, I sought refuge in Santiago's beautiful parks and gardens. The Parque Forestal, with its lush greenery and meandering pathways, provided a tranquil escape from the city's bustle. I strolled along its shaded avenues, pausing to admire the statues and sculptures that adorned the park, each one telling a story of Santiago's history and artistic legacy.

The Parque Metropolitano, sprawling across the hills that embraced the city, offered a breathtaking panorama of Santiago's skyline. Ascending the funicular to the top of Cerro San Cristobal, I was rewarded with sweeping views that stretched to the horizon. The city unfolded below, its mosaic of buildings and bustling streets reminding me of the vibrant tapestry of life that Santiago held.

In the evenings, I sought out Santiago's culinary delights, venturing into local markets and restaurants that teased my taste buds with tantalizing flavors. From the sizzle of sizzling empanadas to the delicate balance of ceviche, each dish was a celebration of Chilean cuisine's rich diversity. The warmth and hospitality of the locals added an extra layer of flavor to every meal, their genuine smiles and passion for their culinary traditions making each dining experience truly memorable.

As my journey in Santiago drew to a close, I reflected on the myriad of places I had visited and the experiences that had shaped my time in this captivating city. Santiago had unveiled its treasures, inviting me to explore its historical landmarks, indulge in its culinary delights, and immerse myself in its vibrant arts and culture.

But it was the intangible moments—the connections forged with locals, the laughter shared with fellow travelers, and the sense of wonder that accompanied every new discovery—that truly left an indelible mark on my heart. Santiago had not just been a city to visit; it had become a place of memories, a tapestry of experiences that would forever be woven into the fabric of my travel story.

As I bid farewell to Santiago, I carried with me a newfound appreciation for its beauty, a deeper understanding of its people and culture, and a longing to return one day to relive the magic that had unfolded within its borders. Santiago, with its vibrant energy and captivating allure, had become a cherished chapter in the grand adventure of my life.

<u>Visitation to Plaza Egaña</u>

As the sun bathed the city of Santiago in its warm embrace, I embarked on a shopping adventure that would take me to the vibrant Plaza Egaña. Nestled in the La Reina neighborhood, this modern shopping plaza beckoned with promises of retail delights and a world of possibilities.

As I approached Plaza Egaña, the sleek, contemporary architecture caught my eye, setting the stage for the shopping experience that awaited me. The entrance welcomed me with wide glass doors, leading me into a realm of retail paradise.

Stepping inside, I was immediately greeted by a lively atmosphere and a symphony of bustling shoppers. The spacious interior of Plaza Egaña revealed a world of retail wonders. From renowned fashion brands to specialty stores, there was an abundance of choices to suit every taste and style.

With a shopping list in hand and a heart full of anticipation, I embarked on my journey through the plaza. The vibrant displays of fashion boutiques enticed me with their chic designs and stylish ensembles. I found myself drawn to the latest trends, admiring the impeccable craftsmanship and attention to detail that adorned the racks and mannequins.

As I perused the stores, the friendly and knowledgeable staff stood ready to assist, their genuine smiles adding a personal touch to the shopping experience. They shared insights about the latest collections, helping me find the perfect pieces that would reflect my individuality and style.

Plaza Egaña wasn't just about fashion; it was a treasure trove of retail offerings. Electronics stores showcased the latest gadgets and cutting-edge technology, tempting me with their innovative features and sleek designs. The vibrant displays of smartphones, tablets, and home entertainment systems filled me with a sense of wonder and sparked my curiosity to explore the possibilities of the digital world.

Moving through the plaza, I discovered an array of specialty stores catering to unique interests and passions. A bookstore enticed me with its shelves overflowing with literary treasures, inviting me to immerse myself in the world of words and imagination. A home decor boutique captivated my attention with its exquisite furnishings and stylish accents, inspiring ideas for transforming living spaces into havens of comfort and beauty.

As my shopping journey progressed, hunger pangs beckoned me to indulge in the culinary delights that Plaza Egaña had to offer. The aroma of freshly brewed coffee permeated the air, leading me to a cozy café where I savored each sip, savoring the rich flavors and enjoying a moment of respite amidst the shopping frenzy. From casual dining options to gourmet delights, the plaza's diverse selection of eateries catered to every craving, offering a delightful interlude to recharge and refuel.

Plaza Egaña wasn't just a shopping destination; it was a hub of entertainment. I found myself drawn to the vibrant cinema complex, where the latest blockbuster movies awaited. The plush seats and state-of-the-art screens transported me to far-off worlds, evoking laughter, tears, and moments of pure cinematic magic.

As the day wore on, I carried my shopping bags filled with newfound treasures, each item a reminder of the delightful experience I had at Plaza Egaña. The bustling energy of the plaza, the personalized service, and the sheer variety of retail options had exceeded my expectations.

Leaving the plaza, I couldn't help but reflect on the memories created during my visit. Plaza Egaña had become more than just a shopping destination; it had woven itself into the tapestry of my travel story. The excitement of finding that perfect outfit, the thrill of discovering unique treasures, and the joy of connecting with the vibrant spirit of Santiago's retail scene had left an indelible mark on my heart.

As I bid farewell to Plaza Egaña, I carried not just shopping bags but a collection of memories. Memories of a day well spent, of a shopping adventure that had ignited my senses and fulfilled my desires. Plaza Egaña had provided me with a captivating retail experience, reminding me of the joy and thrill that can be found within the realms of a modern shopping plaza

VISITATION TO ZOO.

The sun-drenched city of Santiago, Chile, held within its heart a haven of biodiversity and captivating creatures. On a bright and cheerful day, I set out to explore the renowned Santiago Zoo, eager to encounter the wonders of the animal kingdom.

As I stepped into the lush surroundings of the zoo, a symphony of sounds greeted my ears. The chirping of birds, the rustling of leaves, and the distant roars and calls of exotic creatures created an atmosphere brimming with anticipation. I found myself immersed in a world where the beauty and diversity of nature were showcased before my very eyes.

The first exhibit I encountered was a majestic habitat of big cats. I stood in awe as I beheld the graceful movements of sleek cheetahs, the regal presence of noble lions, and the powerful stride of elusive jaguars. Their golden eyes seemed to hold a depth of wisdom, and I couldn't help but feel a sense of reverence for these magnificent creatures that ruled their domains with grace and strength.

Moving on, I entered a tropical paradise, where vibrant colors and the intoxicating fragrance of flowers surrounded me. In this haven, I encountered a kaleidoscope of avian wonders. Tropical birds, with their striking plumage, fluttered overhead, their melodic calls adding a melodic soundtrack to the scenery. Scarlet macaws, graceful toucans, and playful parrots captured my attention, and I marveled at their vibrant feathers and lively personalities.

As I ventured further into the depths of the zoo, I encountered a menagerie of creatures from around the globe. From the regal elephants that seemed to exude wisdom and strength, to the mischievous monkeys swinging from branch to branch, each animal told a story of resilience, adaptability, and the remarkable diversity of life on our planet.

The underwater wonders of the aquarium mesmerized me, as schools of shimmering fish gracefully glided through their aquatic world.

The vibrant coral reefs, teeming with life, were a reminder of the delicate balance that exists beneath the ocean's surface. I watched in awe as graceful sea turtles swam by, their gentle movements reflecting a sense of serenity and ancient wisdom.

A highlight of my visit was encountering the gentle giants of the zoo: the magnificent elephants. Their sheer size and gentle demeanor evoked a sense of awe and wonder. I observed as they playfully interacted with each other, their trunks reaching out to touch, and their eyes revealing an intelligence and emotional depth that left me humbled.

As I navigated the winding paths of the zoo, I couldn't help but appreciate the efforts dedicated to conservation and education. Informative signs and displays provided insights into the conservation challenges faced by these animals, reminding visitors of the importance of protecting their habitats and promoting their well-being.

Leaving the Santiago Zoo, I carried with me a profound appreciation for the marvels of the natural world. The experience had deepened my connection to the animal kingdom, fostering a sense of responsibility to safeguard these magnificent creatures and the ecosystems they call home.

The memories of the zoo lingered within me, a vivid tapestry of encounters with captivating creatures and a renewed understanding of our interconnectedness with the animal world. The Santiago Zoo had not only provided me with a day of wonder and fascination, but it had also ignited a flame of curiosity and conservation within my heart, inspiring me to champion the preservation of our planet's precious wildlife.

Visitation to museum

In the heart of Santiago, Chile, I embarked on a journey through time and art, guided by the doors of a prestigious museum. With anticipation and curiosity, I stepped into a world where history, culture, and creativity converged—a place that would forever leave an indelible mark on my soul.

As I entered the museum, I was greeted by a grand hall adorned with towering columns and magnificent artwork. The air was filled with an atmosphere of reverence and awe. The hushed whispers of visitors mingled with the sound of soft footsteps, creating a symphony of anticipation.

My exploration began in the historical exhibits, where artifacts from ancient civilizations transported me back in time. From intricate pottery and exquisite sculptures to intricate tapestries and ancient artifacts, each item held within its essence a story waiting to be told. I marveled at the skill and artistry of these ancient civilizations, their legacies preserved in the halls of the museum.

Moving through the gallery, I found myself surrounded by the masterpieces of renowned artists. Paintings adorned the walls, showcasing a kaleidoscope of colors, emotions, and perspectives. The strokes of brush and palette knife came to life before my eyes, breathing soul into canvases that had stood the test of time. I immersed myself in the works of iconic artists, experiencing the profound impact of their creative expressions.

As I continued my exploration, I stumbled upon a hall dedicated to contemporary art. Here, I encountered thought-provoking installations, abstract creations, and avant-garde pieces that challenged conventional boundaries. The museum's commitment to showcasing the evolution of art was evident, as it celebrated both traditional and cutting-edge forms of expression.

One of the highlights of my visit was an exhibition showcasing the rich cultural heritage of Chile. The vibrant colors and intricate patterns of indigenous art captivated my senses, telling stories of ancestral traditions and the resilience of indigenous communities. I felt a deep connection to the land and its people as I immersed myself in the tapestries of history woven within the fabric of Chilean culture.

The museum was not just a repository of art; it was a sanctuary of knowledge. I found myself drawn to the educational displays that offered insights into scientific discoveries, historical events, and cultural phenomena. Interactive exhibits sparked my curiosity and encouraged me to engage with the subjects on a deeper level, expanding my understanding of the world around me.

As I concluded my museum journey, I reflected on the vastness of human creativity, the power of art to transcend time and space, and the profound impact it has on our collective consciousness. The museum had offered me a glimpse into the depths of human imagination and a window into the richness of Chilean history and culture.

Leaving the museum, I carried with me a sense of awe and inspiration. The stories and visions I had encountered within those walls had ignited a fire within my own creative spirit. The museum had become more than a space to behold art; it had become a catalyst for personal growth and a reminder of the boundless potential of the human mind.

With each step back into the vibrant streets of Santiago, I carried the echoes of the museum within me. Its corridors of art, history, and knowledge had become a part of my own narrative, enriching my understanding of the world and leaving an everlasting imprint on my journey through life. The museum had become a sacred space—a sanctuary where the human spirit found solace, inspiration, and the timeless beauty of human expression.

BEAUTIFUL THINGS I SAW

Within the enchanting halls of the museum, my eyes beheld a myriad of breathtaking and captivating treasures. Here are some of the beautiful things I encountered during my visit:

1. Masterful Paintings: The museum boasted an impressive collection of paintings that spanned centuries of artistic brilliance. From the ethereal brushstrokes of renowned Impressionist works to the bold and vibrant colors of modern masterpieces, each canvas unveiled a world of emotions and stories. I was mesmerized by the delicate play of light in landscapes, the tender expressions on portraits, and the evocative symbolism in abstract art.

2. Intricate Sculptures: Sculptures stood like silent sentinels, their forms carved with meticulous precision. I marveled at the way artists brought life to stone and metal, capturing the grace of the human body and the essence of mythical creatures. The interplay of textures, the flowing drapery, and the sheer craftsmanship held me in awe, allowing me to appreciate the power of three-dimensional art.

3. Ancient Artifacts: The museum's collection of ancient artifacts transported me to distant civilizations and epochs. I encountered

delicately painted pottery adorned with intricate patterns, exquisitely carved religious statues that whispered tales of devotion, and ancient tools that spoke of human ingenuity. Each artifact carried the weight of history, offering glimpses into the customs, beliefs, and artistic sensibilities of our ancestors.

4. Mesmerizing Jewelry: Glittering jewels and precious metals sparkled under the soft museum lights, showcasing the artistry of jewelry design throughout the ages. Adorned with shimmering gemstones and intricate metalwork, the pieces exuded elegance and timeless beauty. I marveled at the

craftsmanship and the stories they held, imagining the celebrations, romances, and legacies woven into each precious artifact.

5. Textile Treasures: A feast for the senses awaited me in the textile exhibits. Elaborate tapestries unfolded before my eyes, their intricate weaves telling tales of historical events and mythological narratives. The vibrant colors and meticulous details were a testament to the skill and patience of the artisans who wove them. I found myself immersed in the tactile beauty of richly embroidered garments, appreciating the artistry and cultural significance they embodied.

6. Exquisite Ceramics: The delicate art of ceramics graced the museum's galleries, showcasing the boundless creativity of human hands. I marveled at the intricately painted vases, bowls, and figurines that adorned the displays. The harmonious blending of colors, the precision of brushstrokes, and the flawless glazing spoke of an ancient tradition preserved

through time, inviting me to appreciate the artistry and craftsmanship behind each piece.

These were just a few of the many beautiful things that filled the museum's halls, each one a testament to human creativity, cultural heritage, and the enduring power of artistic expression. The museum offered a sanctuary where beauty converged with history and culture, allowing me to witness the timeless wonders created by the hands and hearts of countless artists throughout the ages.

CHAPTER SIX

Rules and regulations

I embraced the opportunity to immerse myself in the local culture and abide by the rules and regulations that govern this vibrant city. Respectful and mindful of my surroundings, I understood the importance of adhering to these guidelines, not only for my own safety but also to contribute to the well-being of the community.

Here is a story of the rules and regulations I followed during my visit:

Upon my arrival in Santiago, I familiarized myself with the local laws and regulations, seeking to be a responsible visitor in this beautiful city. I made it a point to respect the customs and traditions of the local culture, always mindful of the impact my actions could have on others.

I began by ensuring I had all the necessary travel documents in order. I carried a valid passport and any required visas, keeping them securely in a designated pouch. This allowed me to navigate the city confidently, knowing that I was in compliance with the immigration regulations.

In terms of transportation, I familiarized myself with the local traffic laws. I followed the designated traffic signals and crossed the streets at designated crosswalks, ensuring my safety and that of others. When using public transportation, such as buses or the metro, I observed the rules and regulations set forth by the transport authorities, including giving up my seat to those in need and keeping my belongings secure.

Respecting the environment was a priority during my visit. I made a conscious effort to dispose of my waste properly, utilizing designated trash bins and recycling facilities. I refrained from littering and actively sought out ways to minimize my ecological footprint, such as conserving water and energy in accommodations.

When exploring the city's landmarks, parks, and public spaces, I followed the guidelines and regulations set by the local authorities. This included adhering to designated visiting hours, respecting any restricted areas or closures, and refraining from causing any damage to the natural or cultural heritage of the sites.

Respecting the local customs and traditions was also essential. I dressed modestly when visiting religious sites or participating in cultural events, ensuring I was appropriately attired out of respect for the local customs. I refrained from engaging in behavior that could be deemed disrespectful or offensive to the local community, always aiming to foster a sense of cultural understanding and appreciation.

Lastly, I engaged in responsible tourism practices by supporting local businesses and communities. I sought out locally owned establishments, restaurants, and artisans, contributing to the local economy and cultural preservation. I embraced the local customs, traditions, and cuisines, immersing myself in the richness of the Chilean culture.

By following these rules and regulations, I not only had a memorable and fulfilling experience in Santiago but also contributed to the preservation of the city's heritage and the well-being of its residents. I left Santiago with a deep appreciation for the importance of respecting the rules and regulations of any destination, recognizing the positive impact it has on the overall travel experience and the communities we visit.

Rules and regulations in Santiago

1. Carry a valid form of identification, such as your passport, at all times.

2. Respect local customs and traditions.

3. Observe traffic laws and regulations, including speed limits and seatbelt usage.

4. Cross streets at designated crosswalks and follow pedestrian signals.

5. Dispose of waste properly in designated trash bins and recycling containers.

6. Adhere to smoking regulations, which prohibit smoking in enclosed public spaces.

7. Consume alcohol responsibly and follow legal drinking age limits.

8. Respect designated quiet hours and avoid creating excessive noise.

9. Follow any restrictions on alcohol consumption in public areas.

10. Familiarize yourself with emergency contact numbers and procedures.

11. Adhere to immigration regulations and carry necessary visas or permits.

12. Be cautious of pickpocketing and keep your personal belongings secure.

13. Respect wildlife and adhere to guidelines for interacting with animals.

14. Dress modestly when visiting religious sites or participating in cultural events.

15. Follow guidelines for photography in museums, historical sites, and cultural venues.

16. Adhere to designated visiting hours at museums and other attractions.

17. Use authorized currency exchange services or banks to convert money.

18. Observe any regulations or guidelines regarding protected natural areas or parks.

19. Comply with the rules and regulations of public transportation systems.

20. Respect historical sites, monuments, and cultural heritage.

21. Abide by laws regarding the possession and use of illegal drugs and substances.

22. Adhere to designated smoking and non-smoking areas.

23. Familiarize yourself with emergency evacuation procedures at your accommodation.

24. Use licensed and reputable taxis or rideshare services for transportation.

25. Obtain necessary permits or permissions for specific activities, such as hiking or camping.

26. Follow any restrictions on drone usage in public spaces or protected areas.

27. Observe any regulations regarding swimming or water activities in rivers or lakes.

28. Be mindful of your behavior in public spaces and avoid disturbing others.

29. Adhere to guidelines for responsible tourism practices and support local businesses.

30. Respect local laws and regulations regarding public demonstrations or protests.

31. Do not deface or damage any artifacts, structures, or archaeological sites.

32. Comply with regulations regarding the collection or exportation of cultural artifacts.

33. Follow guidelines for responsible and sustainable fishing practices, if applicable.

34. Respect designated parking rules and avoid parking in restricted areas.

35. Familiarize yourself with rules and regulations of specific recreational activities, such as skiing or biking.

36. Follow guidelines for safe and responsible hiking or trekking in natural areas.

37. Use designated camping areas and adhere to regulations for fire safety.

38. Observe regulations regarding the use of public restrooms and facilities.

39. Follow any restrictions on the use of public spaces for recreational activities.

40. Respect rules and regulations set by tour operators or guides during excursions.

41. Adhere to any restrictions on the use of audio or video recording devices in certain locations.

42. Follow guidelines for responsible water usage and conservation.

43. Be aware of any restrictions or regulations regarding drone usage or aerial photography.

44. Respect regulations regarding the use of public transportation during peak hours.

45. Comply with regulations regarding the consumption or possession of open alcoholic beverages in public.

46. Follow guidelines for responsible waste management and recycling.

47. Respect regulations regarding the protection of endangered or protected species.

48. Adhere to regulations regarding the use of public parks and recreational areas.

49. Follow any guidelines or regulations for participating in adventure sports or outdoor activities.

50. Comply with local laws and regulations to ensure a safe and enjoyable visit for yourself and others.

CHAPTER SEVEN
HOW TO BECOME A CITIZEN

Once upon a time, in the bustling city of Santiago, Chile, I embarked on a life-changing journey to become a citizen of this vibrant and captivating country. It was a path filled with challenges, growth, and a deep connection to the land and its people.

My adventure began when I first set foot in Chile, captivated by its rich culture, breathtaking landscapes, and warm-hearted people. Intrigued by the idea of calling this place my home, I decided to explore the possibility of becoming a citizen, seeking a deeper connection and a sense of belonging.

The first step on this transformative journey was to establish residency in Chile. I diligently researched the various visa options available and found the one that best suited my circumstances. With determination in my heart, I completed the necessary paperwork, gathered the required documents, and submitted my application to the Chilean authorities.

Over time, my roots began to take hold in Santiago. I embraced the language and culture, immersing myself in the vibrant tapestry of Chilean life. I studied the language diligently, attending language classes and conversing with locals to improve my fluency. Through each interaction, I discovered the warmth and hospitality of the Chilean people, who welcomed me with open arms.

As the years passed, my residency status evolved into permanent residency. This milestone marked a significant turning point on my path to citizenship. It was a testament to my commitment to this country, a testament to the bonds I had forged with its people and the love I had developed for its culture and heritage.

To solidify my ties to Chile, I embraced the opportunity to deepen my knowledge of the country's history, values, and civic responsibilities. I eagerly enrolled in integration courses that delved into Chilean history, politics, and social dynamics. The courses not only provided valuable insights into the nation's past but also encouraged me to reflect on my role as a future citizen, nurturing a profound sense of civic duty and responsibility within me.

The day arrived when I felt ready to take the final step on my citizenship journey. Armed with a deep sense of gratitude and respect for Chile, I submitted my application for citizenship. I poured my heart into the application, detailing my experiences, connections, and aspirations for the future. It was an emotional moment, a culmination of years of dedication, learning, and personal growth.

The authorities carefully reviewed my application, assessing my commitment to the country and evaluating my integration efforts. Interviews were conducted, background checks were performed, and my story was woven into the tapestry of those who had walked this path before me. It was a time of anticipation and reflection, as I awaited the decision that would shape my future.

Finally, the long-awaited moment arrived. I received the news that my application had been approved. Waves of joy and gratitude washed over me as I realized that I would soon become a citizen of Chile, forever tied to its land, its culture, and its people.

In a solemn ceremony filled with pride and celebration, I took the oath of allegiance, officially becoming a citizen of Santiago, Chile. It was a moment that will forever be etched in my memory—a testament to the power of determination, resilience, and the indomitable spirit of those who seek to call a new land home.

As a citizen, I embraced my newfound rights and responsibilities. I participated actively in the democratic process, contributed to my local community, and celebrated the diversity that enriches this nation. I became an ambassador for Chile, sharing its beauty, its traditions, and its welcoming spirit with the world.

Becoming a citizen of Santiago, Chile was more than just obtaining a piece of paper—it was a profound transformation of my identity, a fusion of cultures and values that would forever shape my perspective on life. It was a testament to the power of dreams, the resilience of the human spirit, and the boundless possibilities that unfold when we open our hearts to new horizons.

And so, with gratitude in my heart and the spirit of adventure guiding my steps, I embraced my new citizenship as a cherished chapter in the story of my life—a story forever intertwined with the rich tapestry of Santiago, Chile.

DOCUMENTS NEEDED TO BECOME A CITIZEN

1. Passport: A valid passport is typically required as proof of identity and nationality.

2. Birth Certificate: Your original birth certificate or a certified copy, demonstrating your place and date of birth.

3. Marriage Certificate: If applicable, a certified copy of your marriage certificate.

4. Criminal Record Certificate: A document verifying your criminal record or a declaration stating that you have no criminal record.

5. Residency Documentation: Documents demonstrating your legal residency status in Chile, such as a valid visa or residency permit.

6. Proof of Residency: Documents proving your period of residency in Chile, such as rental agreements, utility bills, or bank statements.

7. Work Permits: If you have been working in Chile, relevant work permits and employment history may be required.

8. Language Proficiency Certificate: A certificate or proof of Spanish language proficiency, such as a language course completion certificate or language test results.

9. Integration Course Certificates: Certificates of completion or attendance for integration courses on Chilean history, culture, and civic responsibilities.

10. Chilean Tax Identification Number (RUT): Your RUT number, issued by the Chilean Internal Revenue Service (Servicio de Impuestos Internos).

11. Proof of Income: Documentation showing your financial stability and ability to support yourself, such as bank statements or employment contracts.

12. Health Insurance: Proof of health insurance coverage in Chile, either through private insurance or the public healthcare system.

13. Proof of Social Security Contributions: If applicable, documents showing your contributions to the Chilean social security system.

14. Proof of Education: Educational certificates or transcripts, especially if they contribute to your integration efforts or professional background.

15. Certificate of Good Conduct: A document from your home country or previous places of residence certifying your good conduct and character.

16. Chilean Identification Card (Cédula de Identidad): If you already have a Chilean ID card, it may be required as proof of residency.

17. Proof of Chilean Bank Account: Documentation confirming the opening of a bank account in Chile.

18. Proof of Address: Documents demonstrating your current address in Chile, such as utility bills or rental agreements.

19. Proof of Chilean Social Integration: Documentation or testimonials from community organizations or Chilean residents affirming your integration efforts.

20. Citizenship Application Form: The completed application form for Chilean citizenship, which can be obtained from the Chilean immigration authorities.

CHAPTER EIGHT

191 SPANISH WORDS FOR COMMUNICATION

200 common words in Spanish along with their English meanings

1. Hola - Hello

2. Adiós - Goodbye

3. Sí - Yes

4. No - No

5. Gracias - Thank you

6. Por favor - Please

7. Perdón - Excuse me, I'm sorry

8. De nada - You're welcome

9. Bien - Well, good

10. Mal - Bad

11. Amor - Love

12. Familia - Family

13. Amigo/a - Friend

14. Casa - House

15. Trabajo - Work

16. Escuela - School

17. Comida - Food

18. Agua - Water

19. Tiempo - Time, weather

20. Día - Day

21. Noche - Night

22. Calle - Street

23. Ciudad - City

24. País - Country

25. Viaje - Trip

26. Salud - Health

27. Dinero - Money

28. Tarde - Afternoon, evening

29. Mañana - Morning, tomorrow

30. Feliz - Happy

31. Triste - Sad

32. Grande - Big, large

33. Pequeño/a - Small, little

34. Nuevo/a - New

35. Viejo/a - Old

36. Bueno/a - Good

37. Malo/a - Bad

38. Fácil - Easy

39. Difícil - Difficult

40. Bonito/a - Pretty, beautiful

41. Feo/a - Ugly

42. Interesante - Interesting

43. Aburrido/a - Boring

44. Alto/a - Tall, high

45. Bajo/a - Short, low

46. Rápido/a - Fast, quick

47. Lento/a - Slow

48. Joven - Young

49. Viejo/a - Old

50. Fuerte - Strong

51. Débil - Weak

52. Cálido/a - Warm

53. Frío/a - Cold

54. Cerca - Near

55. Lejos - Far

56. Dentro - Inside

57. Fuera - Outside

58. Derecha - Right

59. Izquierda - Left

60. Arriba - Up

61. Abajo - Down

62. Ayer - Yesterday

63. Hoy - Today

64. Mañana - Tomorrow

65. Ahora - Now

66. Siempre - Always

67. Nunca - Never

68. A veces - Sometimes

69. Tarde - Late

70. Temprano - Early

71. Primero/a - First

72. Último/a - Last

73. Comer - To eat

74. Beber - To drink

75. Dormir - To sleep

76. Trabajar - To work

77. Estudiar - To study

78. Hablar - To speak, to talk

79. Escuchar - To listen

80. Ver - To see

81. Mirar - To look

82. Entender - To understand

83. Saber - To know

84. Querer - To want, to love

85. Amar - To love

86. Sentir - To feel

87. Pensar - To think

88. Creer - To believe

89. Vivir - To live

90. Ir - To go

91. Venir - To come

92. Hacer - To do, to make

93. Dar - To give

94. Tomar - To take

95. Llevar - To carry, to wear

96. Poner - To put, to place

97. Sacar - To take out, to remove

98. Comprar - To buy

99. Vender - To sell

100. Escoger - To choose

101. Quemar - To burn

102. Correr - To run

103. Caminar - To walk

104. Nadar - To swim

105. Saltar - To jump

106. Llover - To rain

107. Nevar - To snow

108. Abrir - To open

109. Cerrar - To close

110. Empezar - To start, to begin

111. Terminar - To finish, to end

112. Gustar - To like

113. Odio - To hate

114. Necesitar - To need

115. Esperar - To wait, to hope

116. Ayudar - To help

117. Cuidar - To take care of

118. Viajar - To travel

119. Conducir - To drive

120. Aprender - To learn

121. Enseñar - To teach

122. Leer - To read

123. Escribir - To write

124. Verificar - To check, to verify

125. Corregir - To correct

126. Resolver - To solve

127. Comprender - To understand

128. Explicar - To explain

129. Memorizar - To memorize

130. Recordar - To remember

131. Olvidar - To forget

132. Probar - To try, to taste

133. Preparar - To prepare

134. Cocinar - To cook

135. Compartir - To share

136. Celebrar - To celebrate

137. Bailar - To dance

138. Cantar - To sing

139. Jugar - To play

140. Reír - To laugh

141. Llorar - To cry

142. Sonreír - To smile

143. Viajar - To travel

144. Nadar - To swim

145. Soñar - To dream

146. Crear - To create

147. Imaginar - To imagine

148. Explorar - To explore

149. Conocer - To know, to be familiar with

150. Amigos - Friends

151. Fiesta - Party

152. Música - Music

153. Baile - Dance

154. Libro - Book

155. Película - Movie

156. Arte - Art

157. Naturaleza - Nature

158. Playa - Beach

159. Montaña - Mountain

160. Parque - Park

161. Museo - Museum

162. Escuela - School

163. Hospital - Hospital

164. Restaurante - Restaurant

165. Café - Coffee

166. Mercado - Market

167. Tienda - Store, shop

168. Cine - Cinema, movie theater

169. Estadio - Stadium

170. Aeropuerto - Airport

171. Autobús - Bus

172 Hola - Hello

173 Adiós - Goodbye

174 Gracias - Thank you

175 Por favor - Please

176 Sí - Yes

177 No - No

178 Amor - Love

179 Amigo/a - Friend

180 Casa - House

181 Comida - Food

182 Agua - Water

183 Tiempo - Time, weather

184. Día - Day

185 Noche - Night

186 Calle - Street

187 Ciudad - City

188 Trabajo - Work

189 Escuela - School

190 Padre - Father

191 Madre - Mother

Made in the USA
Columbia, SC
29 August 2023